Business Pl

in the

Public Sector

Second Edition

Essential Skills for the Public Sector

 PUBLICATIONS

Jennifer Bean
Lascelles Hussey

HB PUBLICATIONS
(Incorporated as Givegood Limited)

Published by:

HB Publications
London, England

First Published 1997 © HB Publications
Second Edition 2011 © HB Publications

British Library Cataloguing in Publication Data

ISBN 978 1 899448 57 9

For further information see www.hbpublications.com
and www.fci-system.com

Contents

Chapter 1

INTRODUCTION

All organisations should plan for the future to establish how to achieve their goals. Successful planning ideally results in the development of a written document; the **business plan**. Business planning has always been essential for the private sector which has to produce business plans for raising funds and supporting requests for borrowing.

Business planning is equally important for the public sector as for the private sector, even though the motivation for undertaking their activities is different. Whereas it is common place for most private sector businesses to maximise profit as the primary objective, the business of the public sector is largely driven by the need to deliver services to fulfil social, political or economic objectives.

In the public sector the term "service or development plan" is sometimes used instead of the term "business plan". In the light of continuing pressure on public services to become more efficient, the business plan is increasingly seen as an important tool which will assist in identifying how service delivery can be maximised given limited or constrained resources.

Business planning is now a common feature within the management of many public services. This book will outline good practice in the development and preparation of business plans, indicating how they should be used both as an internal and external document.

The following chapters set out the important features of business planning, including establishing aims and objectives, the key components of the content, and the financial implications. It should be emphasised, however, that the format of the plan must be individual to the organisation. Although ideas with respect to formats will be given, they **must** be tailored to meet the organisation's needs.

This book is one of a series of "Essential Skills for the Public Sector" titles. The series aims to assist public sector managers become more efficient and effective in carrying out their important management responsibilities. We consider this book to be an important part of the tool kit for public sector management development.

Chapter 2

THE CORPORATE FRAMEWORK

Having a Vision

In order to commence the planning process, it is important to have a vision of what the future of the organisation should be. This vision should encompass all aspects of the organisation including its services, size, culture, and performance. In a commercial enterprise it is normally the proprietors that are responsible for developing the vision and disseminating it throughout the organisation. In the public sector, it is less clear as to who should be responsible for creating and promoting the vision. In many circumstances, it will be the person or group of people at the top of the organisation. This could be the Chief Executive, the management board, or where there is a political environment, as with local authorities, the ruling party. If a group of people are developing the vision, then it should be a shared vision and may require compromises to be made.

The vision is the starting point for any planning and should be kept very simple for ease of communication. In addition, the vision will vary greatly depending on the goals or aspirations of the organisation. For example, a business proprietor may have a vision of the business being a market leader in terms of service quality, whilst a public sector organisation may have the vision of making the service(s) accessible to all members of the community. In both cases, any planning undertaken should be with respect to realising these visions.

Many public sector organisations provide a range of services, and hence having a single simple vision to cover all services sometimes proves difficult. In such cases it may prove easier to concentrate the vision on more general areas such as organisational culture. For example, there may be a vision to be a "responsive" or a "quality" organisation (where quality must be defined). Alternatively, it may be necessary to have different visions for each aspect of the service.

The vision should percolate through to the organisation's mission statement, objectives, policies and procedures, and can sometimes be presented in the form of a "vision statement". Examples of vision statements are given as follows:

> *The Council's overall priority for the period 2010-2015 will be to achieve a recognised improvement in the quality of its services, as defined in the Council's Mission, with an overall budget substantially reducing in real terms.*
>
> **A London Borough**

> *"The public funders of health research are committed to working together to improve the competitiveness of UK health research, speed up the translation of basic science to patient benefit and create an environment attractive to the life sciences industry."*
>
> **A Strategic Health Research Organisation**

Many organisations do not produce a written vision statement due to a range of reasons including the following:

- *Where there is no clear consensus as to who within the organisation should define the vision*

- *Where those at the top of the organisation cannot agree on a common vision*

- *Where activities are so diverse that one vision for the whole organisation is not appropriate*

- *Where the organisation's goals are very changeable making any established vision quickly out of date*

Developing a Mission Statement

A "mission statement" should provide the whole organisation with a common direction. The statement should be based on the organisation's vision, and in some cases, where a vision statement has been developed, the two statements can be the same or overlapping.

The mission statement should contain some of the following important elements

---

DIRECTION

- Where the organisation is going and/or intends to go

- What the organisation does and/or intends to do

- What the organisation is and/or intends to become

PERFORMANCE

- What performance level the organisation intends to achieve

- When the organisation intends to achieve it

MARKET

- Who the organisation provides services for

- The current and/or intended market position

CULTURE

- How the organisation operates and/or intends to operate

- The value system of the organisation

- The skills and abilities of the organisation

Mission statements should also strive to be:

(3M's of Mission Statements)

In order for it to be **meaningful** it has to be accurate and phrased in a way that everyone can understand.

In order for it to be **memorable** it must be relatively brief. Mission statements can vary in length from two words to several sentences. However, most people can only remember one or two sentences at most.

In order for a mission statement to be **motivational** it has to contain a message that everyone in the organisation can relate to, believe in, and support.

Example mission statements are shown below:

> *"To give practicing professionals a learning environment that supports, develops and assists them in enhancing their skills and professionalism in the varied fields related to public management."*
>
> **A University Public Administration Program**

"To enhance the quality of life in the Borough by securing efficient and effective services and promoting the well-being of the community and the Borough's physical environment."

A London Borough

"To work in partnership to provide an excellent, affordable service that will:

Reduce risk throughout the community by protective community safety services, Respond quickly to emergencies with skilful staff, Restore and maintain quality of life in our communities"

A Fire and Rescue Service

A Corporate Framework for Planning

The vision and the mission statements are useful cornerstones for the development of the corporate framework. Some organisations produce a **corporate plan** which sets out the broad strategy within which individual departments, service units, etc. can develop their individual plans. However, even without a corporate plan, a corporate framework is required for planning. This is particularly relevant where the organisation has a number of diverse activities for which plans need to be developed, as is the case with many public sector organisations.

The corporate framework will consist of the following elements:

Where there is no corporate framework, planning may become more difficult as there is no overall guidance or direction provided at the corporate level. Individual departments and units producing business plans are then left to make their own assumptions about direction and develop the plan accordingly.

Having established the vision and mission statement, it is then usual for organisational aims and objectives to be outlined as part of the framework. These will not be directed at particular services but will be more overarching in nature. All other business plans developed within the organisation will have aims and objectives which take into account the corporate ones. The development of aims and objectives are discussed in Chapter 4.

Policies and procedures are developed by organisations to provide consistency in approach to key functions, such as finance, personnel, health and safety, equal opportunities and so on. Some of these will be developed in line with the organisation's vision whilst others will be required by legislation. These provide boundaries for key aspects of the planning process.

Strategic Planning

Strategic planning is usually undertaken at the top of the organisation by the key decision makers. The process sets out the key strategies to be adopted by each service area and the organisation as a whole, and then uses these strategies as part of the business planning process.

The role of strategic planning is to look at the overall approach to be taken in order to achieve the organisational vision and primary goals. It does not set out detailed actions for implementation, but identifies the framework for the development of such action plans. Hence, these strategies often form part of the corporate framework, and can be incorporated into the corporate plan where one is developed.

Examples of key strategies that tend to be developed at this level include the following:

Service Strategy   *To gain quality accreditation for all services*

Human Resource Strategy   *To ensure all staff participate in an appraisal process which identifies staff development needs*

Marketing Strategy   *To raise the profile of the organisation to create greater awareness amongst all customers*

Financial Strategy   *To raise the percentage of total income by charging for certain services*

Technology Strategy   *To enhance all computer systems to maximise efficiency in data processing*

The terms business plan and strategic plan are often used interchangeably. If different plans are to be developed, definitions will be important so that the organisation is clear about the role each will play. Often only one document is produced and titled a **strategic business plan.**

Summary

❏   The vision is the starting point for any planning within the organisation

❏   Many public sector organisations provide a range of services, and it is sometimes difficult to produce a single vision statement

❏   A mission statement should give all those who work within the organisation as well as those external to it, a clear statement setting out how the organisation views itself

❏   The mission statement should strive to be meaningful, memorable and motivational

❏   The strategic planning process sets out the key strategies to be adopted by the organisation and uses this information as the basis for the business planning process

❏   Some of the key strategy areas which are addressed as part of strategic planning include service delivery, human resources, marketing, finance and technology

Exercise 1

Mission Statement

Consider the following mission statements and state whether or not you consider they meet the 3M's.

	Meaningful (✓)	Memorable (✓)	Motivational (✓)
1. To provide a quality service to all our clients	☐	☐	☐
2. To be the best school in the Borough by achieving the highest possible position in the league tables whilst providing equal access for our local children	☐	☐	☐
3. Providing homes; reducing homelessness and creating an environment that people want to live in	☐	☐	☐
4. To serve and protect the whole community with a well trained force that detects crime and enables the individual to live and work in the community without fear	☐	☐	☐
5. To achieve, by March 20XX, sustainable improvement in the physical, economic and social environment of the organisation, improving the quality of life for people who live in, work in and visit the area, creating a model for future regeneration	☐	☐	☐
6. We will care for our patients, our staff and our community by providing the most we can with the resources we are given	☐	☐	☐

	Meaningful (✓)	Memorable (✓)	Motivational (✓)
7. Write the statement of your own organisation, if one exists, and undertake the same test	☐	☐	☐

....

....

....

....

....

....

....

....

....

....

This exercise has been designed to enable the reader to give thought to different types of mission statements as well as their own.

Suggested solutions have not been given due to the subjective nature of the exercise.

Exercise 2

Corporate Framework for Planning

Does your organisation have a corporate framework for planning?

Yes ☐   **No** ☐

If yes, summarise the elements of the framework under the following headings

Vision/Mission

Aims/Objectives

Policies/Procedures

Constraints Affecting Strategy

If no, identify what, if any, key documents exist within the organisation that could contribute to defining the corporate framework. For example, personnel policies and procedures; budget statements; capital expenditure programme; corporate quality standards.

Key Document	Contribution to Corporate Framework

Chapter 3

DEVELOPING A BUSINESS PLAN

Business Planning Process

This is defined as:

"a process whereby an organisation performs a structured appraisal of its objectives; analyses its current position with regard to its activities, resources and the environment in which it operates; and develops actions in order to achieve its objectives."

Within the public sector, the process will often include a wide range of contributors and therefore may take a long time to complete. Ideally, everyone who is affected by the plan should be included in the process in the same way. Otherwise there is a danger that the plan may not be fully supported within the organisation.

Ideally the business planning process should be seen as part of the organisation's management system and can be used to assist in organisational development. It should be emphasised that the process is on-going and so the business plan is subject to change. The business plan will, therefore, require updating throughout its lifetime such that it remains current and accurately reflects the internal and external changes that may be experienced by the organisation.

The stages of the business planning process are shown in the following diagram.

Establish a vision for the organisation which is reflected in a mission statement if applicable
⇩
Set aims that are consistent with the vision and mission
⇩
Develop objectives
⇩
Assess current position of the organisation with respect to current activities, internal and external environment, etc.
⇩
Revisit the objectives to ensure they are still relevant, practical and achievable
⇩
Develop strategies to implement the objectives
⇩
Develop actions to implement strategies
⇩
Link strategies and actions to finance and establish financial requirements to implement plans

The speed of this process can be affected by any of the following:

- *the size of the organisation*
- *the organisational structure*
- *the level to which business planning is devolved, i.e. whether plans are produced for each department or for each service area*

In some cases, the process adopts a bottom up approach where business plans are produced at the lowest level possible and then consolidated up the line throughout the organisation. Alternatively, a top down approach is used whereby parameters for the production of plans are dictated from the top. Ideally, there should be a mixture of the two whereby a corporate framework is developed from the top. Individual service business plans which are consistent with the corporate framework can then be produced, creating a synergy for the organisation as a whole.

Contents of a Business Plan

The content of the plan will vary depending on each organisation's individual requirements, as well as the main purpose for which the plan is being produced. All business plans should be individual and reflect the nature of the organisation to which it pertains, and so headings, layout, content, etc. will differ accordingly.

In order to produce a comprehensive business plan the following areas should be covered:

- *Introduction*
- *Aims and objectives*
- *Description*
- *Management and organisational structure*
- *Market assessment and competitor analysis*
- *Physical resources*
- *Critical analysis*
- *Strategies and detailed action plans*
- *Financial requirements*
- *Financial forecasts*
- *Appendices*

A brief description of what should be included under each of the content headings is set out as follows:

Introduction
This is an important section, especially if the plan is to be seen by third parties as it provides the first impression of the organisation. The introduction should set out briefly the purpose and scope of the plan, along with the vision, and perhaps mission statement. It should also include:

- *relevant aspects of the corporate framework, if applicable*

- *key assumptions that have been made when preparing the plan, such as whether or not competition will apply to the service*

- *key constraints facing the organisation/ service, such as a limited budget*

- *the readership or audience to which it is directed*

- *a brief overview of the content and structure of the rest of the plan*

Aims and objectives

The organisation should set out its aims and objectives early on in the business plan, since the plan will focus on how those aims and objectives are to be achieved. The objectives should be linked with the relevant strategies and actions required for their achievement. Aims and objectives will be discussed in more detail in chapter 4.

Description

The organisation should describe all its activities. This section should include a description of the services provided or products produced; the background to the organisation; the historic track record, emphasising the successes achieved in the past; and may also include summarised information on the historical financial performance of the organisation.

Where possible the description should be linked to quality standards and performance indicators/targets. This will give the reader a clear understanding of the service and the quality to which it is being delivered.

Management and organisational structure

Where a business plan is prepared for fund-raising, this is considered to be one of the most important sections. This is because regardless of what is written in the plan, the quality of the management team will be a significant factor in whether or not the plan is implemented. It is usual to present a diagram of the organisational structure showing reporting lines and lines of authority. Where they exist, it is useful to add links with other agencies especially if such agencies are key to operations.

This section should identify the decision making process, levels of accountability, and the key roles within the organisation. Profiles of the senior management should also be included in the business plan, but these are often included as an appendix.

Market assessment and competitor analysis

The market assessment reflects the market research undertaken by the organisation and its assessment of the market place in which it is operating. This assessment identifies areas such as:

- *the size of the market place*

- *the growth rate*

- *the client groups*

- *the market trends (including potential changes in the market place)*

- *the number of existing providers*

- *the potential for new entrants*

- *the organisation's position within the market place*

Other existing providers may be competitors or collaborators. If they are competitors, the organisation should identify what makes them different, and in particular, any areas of competitive advantage. A competitive advantage represents a benefit to the customer/client over and above that provided by the competition. An organisation may have a competitive advantage on issues such as service quality, the price or the scope or range of services. These competitive advantages can be used in the development of the marketing strategy.

Physical resources

This section should identify all the physical and human resources that are required to deliver the organisation's services. For example, equipment, property, staffing levels, and so on. Where physical resources are very limited, this section may be excluded, and human resource requirements can be included in the section on management and organisational structure.

Critical analysis

It is necessary for the organisation to take a critical look at itself, by identifying areas of strength and weakness. It should also establish any areas of constraint and sensitivity to change. The techniques used to gather information for this section may include a SWOT and/or PEST analysis. These techniques and others are described in chapter 5.

Strategies and detailed action plans

Strategies describe in general how the objectives will be achieved, whereas the action plans set out the detail. The latter should include a description of the tasks to be undertaken, the timescale for their completion, and the person(s) responsible for implementation. All the actions should be linked to an objective such that they are put into context. In some cases it is useful to identify the costs associated with undertaking the action. The action plan provides management with a comprehensive monitoring tool which can be reviewed on a regular basis.

Financial requirements

This section sets out the level of financial resources needed to deliver the business plan, and how those resources will ideally be met. In many cases this amount will be represented by the budget allocation for the service. However, it is often the case that additional funding is required to meet the organisation's objectives. The business plan should always identify how this gap can be filled, i.e. by an additional grant, fund-raising, charging fees, etc.

Financial forecasts

A business plan should always have a financial section, which is where it may sometimes differ from service plans which are used within some organisations; service plans often exclude financial projections. Financial forecasts provide a detailed account of how the operations described in the business plan will affect the organisation's finances. The forecast is normally presented as a month by month income and expenditure forecast, along with a cash flow forecast. These can be used for monitoring purposes throughout the duration of the plan, where the actuals can be compared with the forecasts on an on-going basis.

In order for the reader to understand the forecasts, detailed assumptions need to be included to support the figures. These assumptions should be realistic and based on as much accurate information as possible and where relevant, detailed unit costs may be included.

Financial forecasts and assumptions are frequently included as appendices.

Appendices

In addition to the profiles of key managers, and the financial forecasts and assumptions, there may be a number of other appendices attached to the business plan. These may include marketing information, location diagrams, activity statistics, etc.

Attributes of a Business Plan

Ideally the business plan should possess the following qualities:

- *It should be informative, concise and well presented*
- *It should cover all the criteria that the reader needs to know*
- *It should be usable as a working document and management tool*

A business plan which possesses the above attributes can have a powerful influence on the direction and management of the service. It should be constantly referred to, reviewed and revised as part of the management process. The focus should be to achieve the objectives set out in the plan.

Uses of the Business Plan

A range of uses for the business plan are identified as follows.

As a management tool:
to be used in the day to day management of the organisation

This plan should be comprehensive and include the critical analysis. However, there may be less information on the description and market assessment, and more concentration on the detailed action plans.

As a fund-raising tool:
to be presented to funders

It is likely that this plan will be tailored to meet the funders' requirements, which may be specific in nature. It will also tend to put the organisation in the best possible light, and therefore the critical analysis may not be included or may be edited with respect to some of the weaknesses.

As a promotional tool:
to be distributed to third parties including customers and users

When the business plan is used for marketing purposes, it is often significantly reduced in content compared to a plan used as an internal management tool. It is likely that neither the critical analysis nor the detailed action plan would be included.

As a strategic tool:
to be used by senior and other managers

The business plan can provide the strategic framework for management decision making, and can be communicated to staff to give direction to their activities and a greater understanding of why certain actions have to be taken. There may be less detail to the action plan element, and financial information may be presented in summary form.

Whilst it may be possible to have one document that fulfils all of these requirements, it is quite common for different versions of the business plan to be produced to meet the various needs. Most business plans are confidential as they often include very sensitive information about the organisation. If a business plan is to enter the public domain then any sensitive information should be removed or tailored, and the organisation should ensure there are no issues with respect to data protection.

Summary

❑ The business planning process should ideally be seen as part of the organisation's management system and be used to assist in organisational development

❑ The business planning process can be affected by the size of the organisation, the organisational structure or the level to which business planning is devolved

❑ The content of the business plan will vary depending on the main purposes for which the plan is being developed

❑ The business plan should aim to cover all the criteria that the reader needs to know and be useable as a working document. It should also be informative, concise and well presented

❑ It may be possible to have one document that fulfils a number of requirements, e.g. for management, strategy, fund raising or marketing, although it is quite common for different versions of the plan to be developed for each purpose

Exercise 3

Developing a Business Plan

The local health centre has decided to produce a business plan as part of its bid for additional funds from the local health authority. It was founded a year ago in a purpose built building and provides a range of services to meet the needs of the local community. The budget last year was overspent by 2% as staff training and demand levels had been underestimated. It is predicted that demands on services will increase by 5% over the next two years due to increases in the birth rate, an aging population and higher numbers of asylum seekers coming to the area. Having undertaken market research, it is evident that scope exists to raise some income by introducing charges, however, this is not a desirable option due to the fact that administration costs would also be increased. There is a flat management structure and all staff currently employed are essential to service delivery.

The overall aims of the health centre are to:

☐ Provide flexible community health services which meet local needs

☐ Encourage local participation in the determination of how services are delivered

☐ Provide the highest quality service possible within budgetary constraints

☐ Insist on equality and fairness in the way health services are distributed

☐ Provide a one stop service for all health care information in the local area

☐ Be viewed as a professional and caring organisation by users and staff

With respect to the business plan, the health centre has the following objectives:

☐ To increase income by 10% by way of additional grants

☐ To introduce minimum charges for additional services such as the crèche, the information service and the counselling service

☐ To increase staff numbers by three full time equivalents

☐ To undertake an extensive user survey and issue a public report on the findings

☐ To produce a corporate brochure

☐ To reduce unit costs by 5% by making savings and increasing productivity

☐ To increase staff training days to an average of 5 per person per year

☐ To introduce at least two new service areas based on user demand and local needs

☐ To reduce overall waiting times by an average of 20%

☐ To implement the recommendations from a report "Health Care in the Community" where possible within financial constraints

Given this position, identify what additional information you would require in order to assist in the development of a business plan for the health centre.

....

....

....

....

....

....

....

....

....

....

....

....

....

Suggested solutions to this exercise can be found on page 111.

Exercise 4

Business Planning Process

Using the following table, identify which elements of the business planning process you have undertaken to date.

Stages in the Planning Process	Yes	No	Partly
A clear corporate framework			
Mission statement			
Critical analysis			
Objective setting			
Clear description of activities along with quality standards			
Management and organisational structure			
Development strategies for all areas			
Action plans			
Financial requirements			
Financial forecasts			

To date, are you satisfied with the progress made with respect to the development of the business plan?

Yes ❏   **No** ❏

If no, consider how the planning process needs to be improved or developed further.

....

....

....

....

....

....

....

....

....

....

....

....

Chapter 4

AIMS AND OBJECTIVES

Stating the Aims

It is quite common for some organisations to have a list of **aims** (sometimes called core values), instead of a centralised corporate mission statement.

Examples of such aims are given below:

The City Council aims to be an organisation that:

- *Consults, being open and responsive*

- *Provides quality services using well trained and motivated staff*

- *Reflects the needs of citizens at all times*

- *Is corporate at the point of service delivery*

We will do this by:

- *Continually improving the quality of management*

- *Consulting local people in getting the right services and getting those services right*

- *Recognising our limitations and encouraging partnerships*

- *Attracting and keeping the best (possible) people working for us*

- *Valuing diversity and actively promoting equality of opportunity*

- *Promoting best environmental practice*

- *Councillors and staff working together*

- *Managing and learning from our experiences*

- *Promoting active citizenship*

- *Representing and advocating the aspirations of our citizens and the City itself*

Aims are principles that are on-going for the organisation, i.e. what it would always want to achieve.

Setting the Objectives

To achieve the organisation's aims, it is necessary to develop **objectives** which should be:

Specific
Measurable
Achievable
Realistic
Time-related

If objectives do not meet the SMART criteria, they may be better classified as an aim. Otherwise they should be reviewed and changed until they become SMART. It should be stated that there is often a grey area between aims and objectives and in some cases there may be an element of overlap.

Objectives must be practical in terms of the organisation's resources and must also be sufficiently flexible to meet changes in the organisation's environment.

In general terms, objectives should answer the question "How will we achieve our aims?"

Example objectives for a public sector organisation are given below.

> ### This year we intend to:
>
> - *Decrease staff levels by 2% and improve access to job vacancies*
>
> - *Stimulate and promote business development, enabling100 new businesses to locate in the area*
>
> - *Improve education and training provision by creating 500 new places*
>
> - *Improve road and transport infrastructure to reduce journey times through the City by 15%*
>
> - *Improve housing provision by working in partnership with housing providers to develop 1500 more units*
>
> - *Maintain a high quality environment whereby all forms of pollution are decreased and local nature is preserved*
>
> - *Increase level of community participation through two surveys each year and four public meetings*
>
> - *Achieve maximum productivity and value for money by maintaining monthly monitoring reports for all areas of output*

When developing objectives, it is necessary to cover all key areas of the organisation, such as:

- *service and service delivery*
- *quality*
- *marketing*
- *management and organisational issues*
- *finance and administration issues*

Performance Indicators

Ideally, all organisations should identify appropriate performance indicators that can be measured to assess whether specific targets are being met. Many of these targets will relate to meeting quality standards in respect of service delivery as well as undertaking specific objectives. Performance indicators should ideally reflect **qualitative** and **quantitative** measures, and some examples are given as follows:

Objective/Target		Performance Indicator
Improvements in customer care	➲	Number of complaints
	➲	Satisfaction ratings
Increased productivity	➲	Number of people seen
	➲	Response times
Improved staff morale	➲	More productive hours worked
	➲	Reduced sickness rates

Objective/Target		Performance Indicator
Greater customer awareness	⊃	Increased number of enquiries
	⊃	Higher level of service knowledge by customers
More friendly environment	⊃	Satisfaction ratings
	⊃	Number of complaints

Establishing effective performance indicators will require the setting up of data collection systems, which need to be monitored on a regular basis. Such data analysis is of great benefit to the business planning process.

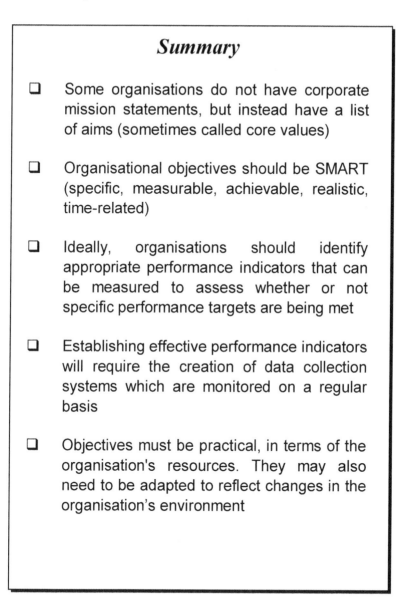

Summary

❑ Some organisations do not have corporate mission statements, but instead have a list of aims (sometimes called core values)

❑ Organisational objectives should be SMART (specific, measurable, achievable, realistic, time-related)

❑ Ideally, organisations should identify appropriate performance indicators that can be measured to assess whether or not specific performance targets are being met

❑ Establishing effective performance indicators will require the creation of data collection systems which are monitored on a regular basis

❑ Objectives must be practical, in terms of the organisation's resources. They may also need to be adapted to reflect changes in the organisation's environment

Exercise 5

Aims and Objectives

Distinguish between the following statements as to which are aims and which are objectives, remembering that objectives should be SMART.

Stages in the Planning Process	AIM? (✓)	OBJECTIVE? (✓)
To provide a responsive service		
To increase quality within financial constraints		
To reduce waiting times by 4% during the year		
To increase income through a fair charging policy		
To introduce means testing for non-essential services within the financial year		
To become the best service provider in the region		
To improve response times to an average of 20 minutes next month		
To create a safer and cleaner environment		
To create 10 new jobs every year		
To develop a quality service meeting the Requirements of international quality standards and obtaining ISO 9000 within the next 24 months		

Suggested solutions to this exercise can be found on page 112

Exercise 6

Setting Objectives

a)   Describe the process by which objectives are established within your organisation

....

....

....

....

....

....

....

....

....

....

....

....

....

b)   List up to 10 objectives you consider your organisation should achieve during the next financial year, and then rank them in order of priority.

	Priority
1) _____	_____
2) _____	_____
3) _____	_____
4) _____	_____
5) _____	_____
6) _____	_____
7) _____	_____
8) _____	_____
9) _____	_____
10) _____	_____

Chapter 5

ORGANISATIONAL ANALYSIS

A number of techniques may be used to develop a picture of the organisation's current position. Some of these techniques are discussed as follows.

SWOT

The SWOT analysis is a commonly used tool to analyse the current position of the organisation, and stands for:

Strengths
Weaknesses
Opportunities
Threats

The SWOT analysis is a process which involves looking at the organisation's current strengths and weaknesses, and identifying any opportunities and threats. The results of the analysis should be taken into account when developing the business plan.

The information for the SWOT analysis can be gathered from a range of sources which include the following:

- *Feedback from staff at all levels*
- *Review of previous business plans*
- *Results of surveys such as customer satisfaction etc.*
- *Quality audit reports*
- *Complaints*
- *Market intelligence*
- *Internal reports and minutes of meetings etc.*

For the SWOT to be most valuable, it should be objective. This may prove difficult to achieve if the process is undertaken entirely internally. Therefore, external parties, such as consultants, may be engaged to assist with the process.

It is important that the SWOT analysis covers all aspects of the organisation, including **service development, marketing, management and organisation, finance and administration.** The SWOT analysis can be defined in the following way:

Strengths

Strengths are aspects which are considered positive and beneficial. For example, a high level of customer satisfaction.

Weaknesses

Weaknesses are factors which require improvement or may be detrimental to the organisation. For example, poor internal communication.

Opportunities

Opportunities are areas of development potential which, if exploited, may bring benefits to the organisation. For example, the opportunity to expand into new market places.

Threats

Threats are issues which present potential disadvantages to the organisation. For example, threats posed by competitors taking away market share.

In order to be of maximum benefit to the business planning process, it is useful to categorise the elements of the SWOT as follows:

Strengths

- *Building blocks:*

  areas which can be used as a basis for strategy development and action plan implementation

- *Competitive advantages:*

  areas in which the organisation does better than the competition; this information can be fed into the marketing strategy

Weaknesses

- *Constraints:*

  areas over which the organisation has little or no control

- *Objectives:*

  areas which can be addressed with clear, "SMART" objectives. These objectives can then be fed into a detailed action plan which will be monitored to ensure weak areas are resolved

Opportunities

• *Fantasy:*

opportunities that sound like good ideas, but cannot be implemented due to constraints or lack of resources. These opportunities are still important as they may become more realistic and achievable in the future

• *Objectives:*

areas that can realistically be exploited. Clear "SMART" objectives and appropriate action plans should be developed such that their achievement can be monitored and measured.

Threats

• *Risks:*

the nature and impact of the threat should be assessed and evaluated. Mitigating actions should be formulated and reflected in the objectives and action plans.

• *Constraints:*

where the risk assessment shows little or no scope for mitigation, the threat becomes a constraint, which will impact on the organisation's plans.

An example of a SWOT analysis is given as follows:

A local fire station is considering developing a business plan for its own internal development and to assist with management. As a starting point, the staff and managers have put together a SWOT analysis and have categorised the points such that they can be utilised in the business planning process. This is shown as follows:

Strengths	Weaknesses
• Committed staff (BB) • Efficient organisation (BB) • Up to date policies and procedures (BB) • Defined catchment area (CA & BB) • New vehicles (CA & BB) • High levels of user satisfaction (CA & BB) • Always respond within minimum response times (CA)	• High level of vacancies (OBJ) • Decreasing budgets (CON) • Lack of leadership (OBJ) • Limited use of IT systems (OBJ) • No regular staff meetings (OBJ) • No formal planning or budgeting process (OBJ) • Inefficient use of staff time, i.e. rotas (OBJ)
Opportunities	Threats
• Implementing staff development plan (OBJ) • Widening range of activities undertaken by the station, e.g. training courses in safety for local businesses (OBJ) • Introduction of time analysis and unit costing (OBJ) • Increasing earned income from third parties by marketing charged for services, obtaining contracts from other areas, etc. (OBJ) • Networking with other stations nationally and internationally (FAN)	• Outsourcing key aspects of the service to private contractors (MIT) • Further reductions in budgets (CON) • Development of independent fire protection services (MIT) • Changes to government legislation with respect to fire services and agencies to deliver fire services (CON) • Low staff morale leading to increased sickness absences (MIT)

Key:	
BB = Building Block for Strategies	CA = Competitive Advantage
CON = Constraint	FAN = Fantasy
OBJ = Objective could be set	MIT = Mitigating objectives/actions

PEST

An organisation's environment consists of a number of factors external to its own marketing system. These factors can be analysed through a process commonly referred to as the PEST analysis:

Political factors
Economic factors
Social factors
Technological factors

Political Factors

Public services operate in a political environment and many decisions are made where political objectives may take priority. Much of the way in which public sector organisations are governed depends on government legislation and elected representatives who exercise local control. Legislation affects the range of services that the public sector can offer and sometimes sets criteria for recipients of the service. Politics and political views will impact on the overall philosophy adopted by the organisation, and the way in which legislation is interpreted.

Economic Factors

The state of the economy affects all organisations including those operating within the public sector. Economic factors such as interest rates, inflation, taxation, and so on, all impact on the income levels of people and organisations. This in turn affects savings, debt, and the availability of credit, grant funding, donations, and public expenditure. Often political decisions are dictated by the economic environment, both national and international. The economic factors that are particularly relevant to the public sector include:

- *Increasing unemployment levels as a result of reduced economic growth*

- *Reduced income arising from grant funding not keeping pace with inflation, and low interest rates on investments*

- *Increasing costs due to high levels of inflation and demand for services, as individual disposable incomes decrease*

Social Factors

Public sector organisations need to take account of social factors that affect their activities and how those activities are perceived. These social factors include issues such as population trends, education, the environment and culture.

Technological Factors

This aspect is concerned with the development of new products and the way in which people work, for example, the use of computer systems. In marketing terms, institutions will often want to emphasise their use of modern equipment and technology, particularly in comparison to their competitors.

Sensitivity

Sensitivity analysis attempts to work through a number of "what if?" scenarios, whereby a particularly sensitive area is subjected to change. An example of this may be in respect of finance:

What if the budget were to be 5% lower than that given last year?

The impact of this scenario on all aspects of the business plan is calculated, identifying how sensitive the organisation is to such a change.

For example, if the budget is cut by 5% there may be a resulting reduction in service by 10%. This may be as a result of lost economies of scale or the loss of key staff responsible for productivity. However, if the budget is cut by 10% it may mean that the organisation is not able to function at all in its current form.

It would be clear from the above example that the organisation is highly sensitive to budget reductions.

Other factors to which an organisation may be particularly sensitive could include:

- *Staff numbers*
- *User numbers*
- *Price changes*
- *Legislation*
- *Competition*

Each of these factors can be analysed to identify the potential level of sensitivity, and their relative impact. This type of analysis establishes the areas of particularly high sensitivity, and can therefore set the parameters within which the organisation should operate in order to achieve its objectives.

Priority Matrix

The priority matrix is another analysis tool which can be used to assist the organisation in establishing its priorities with respect to the objectives and activities to be achieved and undertaken. The matrix comprises a graph with the 'y' axis showing relative importance and the 'x' axis showing relative urgency. The scale for the axis needs to be pre-determined by the organisation and then each objective or activity given a rating for both importance and urgency. When this analysis has been undertaken the information can be plotted on a scatter diagram, which is shown as follows:

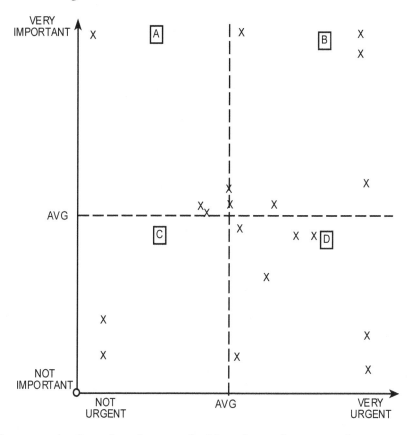

The organisation then has to decide what takes precedence, importance or urgency. Ideally an organisation should focus on what is important rather than urgent, although pressure is often placed on employees to undertake activities that are most urgent.

A matrix can be formed on the given diagram by drawing a line representing the average importance and the average urgency (the dotted lines labelled "AVG" in the priority matrix diagram). If importance takes precedence, then the objectives and activities in boxes A to D should take the following order of priority:

B   *Above average importance and urgency*

A   *Above average importance and below average urgency*

D   *Below average importance and above average urgency*

C   *Below average importance and urgency*

Where urgency takes precedence, the ranking of objectives and activities will change as follows:

B   *Above average urgency and importance*

D   *Above average urgency and below average importance*

A   *Below average urgency and above average importance*

C   *Below average urgency and importance*

Having prioritised objectives and activities, the organisation can then allocate resources and develop implementation plans accordingly.

For example, a school may have preventative health and safety objectives they see as very important but not urgent. If they prioritise importance over urgency, actions relating to these objectives will have a greater priority than those relating to more urgent but less important matters. (such as resurfacing the tennis courts).

The difficulty arises when all the objectives are very important and very urgent. Choices then need to be made as to how resources can be allocated in order to meet the competing priorities.

Summary

❏ The SWOT analysis is a tool regularly used to analyse the current position of the organisation. This process involves identifying an organisation's strengths, weaknesses, opportunities and threats

❏ A PEST analysis can be undertaken to assess the political, economic, social and technological factors which may have an impact on the performance of the organisation

❏ Sensitivity analysis attempts to work through a number of "what if?" scenarios, whereby a particularly sensitive area is subjected to change

❏ The priority matrix can be used to assist the organisation in establishing it's priorities with respect to the objectives and activities to be achieved and undertaken

Exercise 7

Undertaking a SWOT Analysis

You have been asked to undertake a SWOT analysis for a local prison which may be subject to potential competition. The current management are considering an in-house bid for the service, but consider that an independent review would be beneficial as a starting point in helping them decide on a way forward. They have supplied you with the following information:

The prison management team consists of 7 people with clear roles and responsibilities, including the prison governor. They all have a common goal to improve conditions and to increase staff morale. The main inhibiting factor has been a lack of physical and financial resources. Due to a shift in working patterns there has been little time to hold management meetings and communication between managers is considered poor. To date, there has been no time to prepare a business or service plan due to the pressure of work on all staff. Also staff training is not undertaken on any regular basis with the exception of induction training.

Staff have shown high levels of commitment and it is generally considered that they are in support of an in-house bid although no survey has been undertaken to prove this. The prison has been commended on several past occasions for its wide range of activities and educational programmes, along with innovative counselling projects. However, budget cuts have meant that less of this work is now undertaken.

Security systems are very good with up to date technology and the standard of the building is high. The prison is operating at full capacity, although there could be scope to extend the current facilities to provide more places if the appropriate investment is made.

There have been several visits made to the prison by potential private sector providers who would be competitors. These have varied from a local firm to national and international corporations. The current management are concerned that there is no scope for cuts as already there is little waste and productivity is very high. However, it is known that potential privatisation will be seen as a way to reduce expenditure.

The management feel that savings can only be achieved by reducing staff numbers which would have an impact on quality standards such as the security levels and the range of activities currently provided. There is scope to raise income by charging more for the products currently produced in the various workshops, much of which are sold to charitable organisations at cost. Competitors may achieve savings through economies of scale, use of technology, and flexible working if they already have several contracts.

Using this information, complete the following table:

SWOT ANALYSIS

Strengths	Weaknesses
Opportunities	**Threats**

Using your SWOT analysis, consider whether or not the management team should prepare an in-house bid for the contract.

Yes	No
❏	❏

Explain your answer and highlight any areas that will critically affect your decision.

....

....

....

....

....

....

....

....

....

Suggested solutions to this exercise can be found on page 113.

Exercise 8

Undertaking Your Own Organisational Analysis

Undertake your own organisational or service analysis using as many of the tools discussed in the chapter as relevant.

SWOT ANALYSIS

Strengths	Weaknesses
Opportunities	**Threats**

PEST ANALYSIS

Political	Economic
Social	**Technical**

KEY AREAS OF SENSITIVITY

....	....
....	....
....	....
....	....

PRIORITY MATRIX

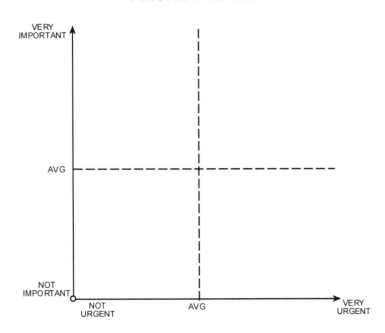

Using the information from all these analysis tools, identify the five key areas of concern that should be addressed by your organisation/service as part of the planning process

1. ....

2. ....

3. ....

4. ....

5. ....

Chapter 6

IMPLEMENTING STRATEGIES AND ACTIONS

Developing Strategies

The business planning process involves developing relevant strategies which the organisation can implement to achieve its objectives. As illustrated in the following diagram, it is a means of getting from A to B.

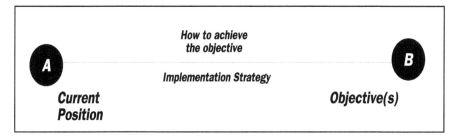

In order to implement strategies, the organisation needs to develop action plans. However, a strategy can be interpreted widely and there is often an overlap between strategies and actions. A useful distinction is to consider that the strategy represents an overall approach and framework to achieve the objectives, whereas actions are specific; similar to the distinction between aims and objectives.

In order to achieve an objective, there may be a number of different strategies that can be adopted. The choice of strategy depends on a number of factors, such as:

The current financial position and the availability of financial resources

In some cases a strategy may require an element of financial input; this may be in the form of capital or revenue expenditure. Depending on the organisation's financial status, some strategies may not be suitable because they are too costly, and unaffordable. The decision as to whether or not to follow a strategy that requires financing should be made on the basis of a cost benefit analysis; that is, do the potential benefits, both tangible and intangible, outweigh the potential costs.

Even if such an analysis is undertaken, and there are clear benefits to be had, a public sector organisation may have limited options regarding access to financial resources. For many organisations, the risks associated with borrowing would be unacceptable, and the choice of strategy will often be limited to what the organisation can afford to implement within normal budgetary parameters.

The available range of skills and abilities within the organisation

The level and type of staff skills and abilities may also be a limiting factor. Certain strategies will depend on knowledge, expertise, and experience, which may or may not be available to the organisation. In some cases external consultants or temporary staff are engaged to bridge the gaps.

The range of available physical resources

Some strategies may require physical resources such as equipment or floor space. For example, a strategy that requires establishing a service specific database may require computer systems with complex capabilities, which the organisation may not have.

The organisational structure and corporate framework

The range of strategic options may be reduced due to limitations and constraints laid down by the organisational structure. This is particularly the case in a large organisation where business planning is devolved to operational units. The strategies identified by each unit may conflict with each other and/or elements of the corporate framework, hence making implementation difficult, or impossible.

The time available for implementation

Time will always be a factor when deciding on which strategic option to adopt. Some strategies will take longer to implement but may be more effective in the long term. The choice of strategy may depend on the importance of timing.

The number and type of objectives that have to be achieved

The business planning process may throw up a number of objectives that need to be achieved. Quite often it is possible to link the objectives such that when certain strategies are implemented, they will assist in achieving more than one objective. The choice of strategy may be affected by the number of objectives it can achieve.

External factors

All organisations are affected by external factors such as legislation, and the economic environment. These factors act as constraints when considering the range of strategic options available.

Most of this information should have been gathered whilst undertaking other elements of the business planning process, such as the critical analysis.

Having identified all this information, the organisation can set out the range of strategies to be considered for each key area of activity. The impact of each strategy will need to be considered when deciding which one will be most appropriate.

Sometimes there are a number of available options, all of which are feasible. In such cases it might be justified to follow several different strategies and through implementation identify which strategy proves to be most effective.

An example of developing strategies in practice is given as follows:

A clinic is developing a business plan for next year and has reached the point where it has to develop its strategies. The organisation has undertaken a SWOT analysis, which has identified the constraints within which it has to work. As this is the first year of business planning, the organisation has set itself the following 5 objectives to be achieved within the financial year.

a) To increase the number of users by 25%
b) To increase the range of services on offer
c) To raise the public profile of the clinic and its services
d) To generate 10% of income from fee charges
e) To gain an accreditation for staff development policies

In order to achieve these objectives, the organisation required a marketing strategy, a service development strategy, a financial strategy and a human resource strategy. There were several options available to the clinic in each area.

The process adopted by the clinic with regard to the marketing strategy is shown as follows:

CURRENT POSITION	OBJECTIVE	MARKETING STRATEGY
• No marketing initiative • Limited customer knowledge of range of services • No understanding of customer satisfaction levels to date • Low public profile	**Raise public profile of the clinic and its services**	• Undertake a user survey to identify customer satisfaction, public image, etc. • Hold open days for target groups • Develop Corporate Literature and website

The strategic options were developed by brainstorming ideas within the business planning team. All options were considered but the ones in the marketing strategy box were those finally agreed upon. Options such as advertising in the local paper were rejected as a result of cost.

A similar process was adopted to create all the other strategies.

Action Planning

Having established the overall strategies to be adopted for each area, the action plan will break down the strategy into tangible action points. These will include timescales that can be monitored throughout the time frame of the business plan. The action plan should state:

- the action to be taken
- the person responsible for ensuring the action is undertaken
- the time within which the action should be completed
- the cost of the action (if applicable), and
- the objective to which the action relates.

Some actions will relate to more than one objective, in which case it should be cross-referred to all the relevant objectives.

An example of action planning in practice is given below.

The clinic referred to earlier, produced a detailed action plan in respect to all their strategies. An extract of the action plan for the marketing strategy is shown as follows:

Action	Person Responsible	Timescale	Cost	Objective
Write, design and print a corporate brochure	LP	May	£2,000	(c)
Develop a new website	LP	July	£3,000	(c)
Distribute brochure to all existing users, local GP surgeries, libraries, public offices, etc.	MB	June Onwards	£1,000	(c), (a)
Arrange an open afternoon every two months	LP	June Onwards	£250 each	(c), (a)
Design a questionnaire for a customer survey	AA	July	-	(c), (a) (b), (d)
Complete the survey and analyse the results	MB	September	-	(c), (a) (b), (d)
Produce a report on survey findings and set targets for improvement	MB	October	-	(c), (a) (b), (d) (e)

The action plan can be very detailed with specific tasks, or can be more general in nature. Again, the level of detail will vary depending upon how the business plan is to be used.

Monitoring Results

To ensure that the business plan is being implemented and to analyse whether the plan is achieving the desired result, it is essential that a monitoring process is established. Given that there is overall commitment to the planning process, the monitoring of the plan can be undertaken at a number of levels within the organisation.

Management should seek to monitor the objectives, the strategy, and the action plan results on a regular basis. Ideally this should coincide with established management meetings and should form a regular agenda item. Detailed monitoring of certain aspects of the plan can also be devolved to staff responsible for implementation.

The monitoring process should include a number of stages as shown by the following flow chart.

The Monitoring Process

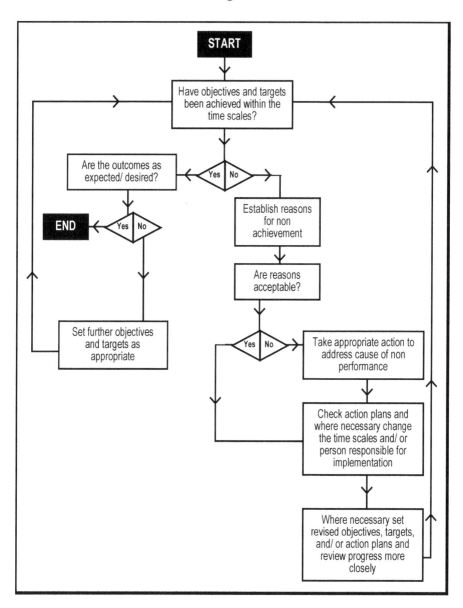

Revising the Plan

A business plan should be monitored on a regular basis, at least monthly, but for some organisations more regular monitoring may be appropriate. The total plan will require review, and perhaps revision on at least an annual basis, even if it is a three or five year plan. This is particularly relevant for public services, where funding is often agreed on an annual basis, and plans may need to change to reflect revised funding levels.

This revision should include:

- *Ensuring that the vision and mission statements are still appropriate and have not been affected by internal or external changes*

- *Checking that the aims are still relevant*

- *Identifying which objectives have been achieved and which have not*

- *Developing new objectives, and transferring the long term objectives to short term objectives where appropriate*

- *Developing new strategies and actions in line with the new objectives*

If there are major changes which make part of the plan redundant, it may be necessary to revise the plan at an earlier stage, say within one year.

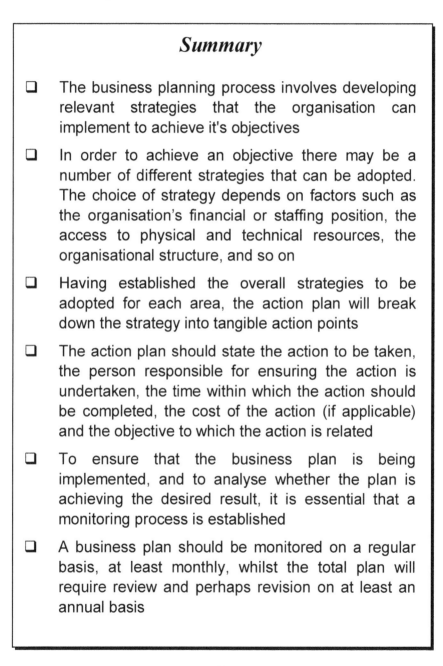

Summary

❑ The business planning process involves developing relevant strategies that the organisation can implement to achieve it's objectives

❑ In order to achieve an objective there may be a number of different strategies that can be adopted. The choice of strategy depends on factors such as the organisation's financial or staffing position, the access to physical and technical resources, the organisational structure, and so on

❑ Having established the overall strategies to be adopted for each area, the action plan will break down the strategy into tangible action points

❑ The action plan should state the action to be taken, the person responsible for ensuring the action is undertaken, the time within which the action should be completed, the cost of the action (if applicable) and the objective to which the action is related

❑ To ensure that the business plan is being implemented, and to analyse whether the plan is achieving the desired result, it is essential that a monitoring process is established

❑ A business plan should be monitored on a regular basis, at least monthly, whilst the total plan will require review and perhaps revision on at least an annual basis

Exercise 9

Developing Strategies

Using the information in exercise 7, identify the strategies that need to be undertaken by the prison's management team

```
┌─────────────────────────────────────────────┐
│                                             │
│         Service Development Strategy        │
│                                             │
│                                             │
│                                             │
│                                             │
│                                             │
│                                             │
└─────────────────────────────────────────────┘
```

```
┌─────────────────────────────────────────────┐
│                                             │
│              Marketing Strategy             │
│                                             │
│                                             │
│                                             │
│                                             │
│                                             │
│                                             │
└─────────────────────────────────────────────┘
```

Human Resource Strategy

Financial Strategy

Suggested solutions to this exercise can be found on page 115.

Chapter 7

PRACTICAL ASPECTS OF PLANNING

Realistic Timescales

The development of an effective business plan may initially take many months, and it is not uncommon for organisations to spend in excess of three months. This is especially the case if the process is to involve all aspects of the organisation. It is therefore necessary to plan how the production of the business plan will proceed. There are two main approaches which can be taken.

Bottom up: *The lowest unit of operation produces a plan which is fed up into higher level plans, until the departmental and corporate plans are developed.*

Top down: *The organisation sets out a strategic corporate plan as a framework, within which all other departments/ divisions/ operational units need to formulate their individual plans.*

There are benefits to both approaches and each organisation must decide which will be most effective based on its own culture. Ideally, both are used, starting with the corporate plan as a framework (top down), followed by the development of departmental plans using a bottom up approach; both allowing for flexibility to accommodate change.

The planning process is continuous and even where plans are developed by an individual in a short timescale, the process can still be a useful one. A plan formulated in this manner can be used as a basis for further development and should be open to change as other people are given an opportunity to feed their ideas into the process.

Steps for business plan development are shown in the following diagram.

1. **Decide on key organisational goals and mission**

2. **Identify methodology of the planning process – top down; bottom up; convergence with budget setting cycle**

3. **Select team responsible for business plan production who will lead the process**

4. **Undertake planning activities, e.g. SWOT analysis, objective setting, etc. with maximum involvement of all stakeholders**

5. **Produce draft plan for open discussion and change**

6. **Finalise document for distribution and implementation**

7. **Review plan on a regular basis and assess results**

Cost

Some organisations obtain outside assistance in order to help with the development of their business plan. This help usually takes the form of an experienced consultant who may be involved with part or all of the process. The consultant can play a role in any of the following activities:

- *Facilitating business planning team*
- *Undertaking SWOT and PEST analysis*
- *Objective setting*
- *Quality standards*
- *Strategy development*
- *Development of financial forecasts*
- *Producing the written document*

Using a consultant can be costly and hence may be prohibitive to some organisations where finance is very limited. However, there are a number of benefits to using an external consultant for assistance. These include:

- *Objectivity*
- *Confidentiality for staff who provide information*
- *Skill and experience*
- *Expert advice on difficult issues*
- *Less demand on management and staff time*
- *Speed of production*

- *A professional approach to the planning process*

The use of consultants can also have some negative results because:

- *Some staff may feel alienated or distanced from the process*
- *The process is seen to be "too professional", and not reflective of the organisational culture*
- *The process may be seen as an "exercise" rather than the development of a useful operational tool*
- *There is a lack of ownership of the end product*

In addition to consultancy costs, other costs which may be incurred include the staff and management time used in developing the plan, and the cost of producing the end document, for example printing and publishing costs.

Business Plan Implementation

Implementation of the business plan is often the most difficult aspect of the business planning process. If the organisation has ensured that all the key people have been involved in the process from the beginning, then the implementation phase is easier as everyone should ideally be committed to the plan. However, it may be that for a number of reasons the process up until this stage has only involved very few people, in which case implementation may be more difficult.

Implementation involves the following steps:

(a) Communicating the contents of the business plan to all staff

It is important that everyone in the organisation regardless of grade, are aware of the aims and objectives that need to be achieved during the year. People are the most important resource when it comes to the delivery of services and therefore each person must be clear of their role with respect to the success of the business plan. This communication can be undertaken by way of an open meeting, small workshop sessions with groups of staff, or on an individual basis. It is often useful to use an outside facilitator if a large meeting has been called to present the plan.

(b) Identifying areas that will require more detailed operational plans to be made

There may be parts of the action plan that require a far more detailed operational plan to be drawn up. One such action may be to produce a marketing plan. This in itself is a task that requires a detailed operational plan. The same process should be undertaken as for business planning but just in relation to marketing. The marketing plan should result in the development of an action plan that details what is going to be done and who is responsible for undertaking the action and when. For example:

ACTION: *Write contents of publicity leaflet*
PERSON: *Admissions officer*
TIME: *By January*

Other operational plans may include the **information technology plan**, the **staff development plan**, the **administrative systems development plan** and so on. It is most common for people with direct responsibility and involvement in these areas to be the main individuals responsible for drawing up these plans. Operational plans will tend to have a short term outlook and require frequent monitoring.

(c) **Communicating how the monitoring processes will take place**

In order for the monitoring process to work successfully, everyone needs to be aware of the process, otherwise it will result in certain pieces of critical data not being collected. For example, all staff should be aware of how often performance assessments are being undertaken, what the quality criteria are, and which key performance indicators are to be monitored.

(d) **Monitoring the outcomes of actions, and monitoring performance**

The action plans can be closely monitored as to whether or not the tasks were carried out within the given timescale. The results of the actions must also be monitored in terms of the various performance indicators that would have been set. Performance should be measured in both *quantitative* and *qualitative* terms, many of which relate back to the original objectives. The business plan cannot be monitored correctly if there is a lack of clarity about the outcomes expected from its implementation.

(e) Explaining how the planning process works

To ensure that everyone is aware of the business planning process and provides input to its preparation (where necessary), it is important that the process for producing the business plan is fully explained. The business plan will be enhanced by the learning process that takes place in the early years of planning.

(f) Ensuring motivation and commitment to making the plan work

The action points in the business plan and the objectives to be achieved require everyone in the organisation to show a certain level of commitment and motivation. If there are issues which may have a negative impact on staff morale, such as the need for staff reductions or budget cuts, managers should ensure staff understand why those decisions have been made. This will assist in maintaining motivation and commitment to implementing the plan.

Presenting and Disseminating the Plan

Once formulated, all members of the organisation, at every level, should have a commitment to the implementation of the business plan. If the business planning process has been correctly undertaken, then there is no reason why this should not happen. However, it is essential that the plan is presented and disseminated to all staff, particularly those who did not have a direct input into its development.

There may also be a need to present the business plan to people outside of the organisation. This may include senior managers, chief officers and chief executives, outside sponsors and funders. This requires a very good working knowledge of all aspects of the plan such that questions can be answered confidently. It may prove useful to summarise the plan by way of key points in relation to each section so that it is clear to those outside the organisation exactly what the objectives are, which services are being provided, and how the objectives are going to be achieved over time. This summary is regularly usually to as an "executive summary".

Business Planning Cycle

Business planning should be an established cycle within the organisation and should, where possible, relate to the budgeting cycle (the timetable for producing the annual budget). In this way, it is possible to tie the objectives, strategies and action plan to the realistic allocation of financial and other resources. The following diagram shows that the planning process should never end, but be on-going as plans are constantly reviewed and evaluated.

Business Planning Cycle

Set Objectives

Reassess the Current Position

Plan how they will be achieved

Evaluate Results

Implement Plan

Monitor Progress

This is an ongoing cycle, guided by the corporate aims/ goals and the external environment.

Dealing with Uncertainty

One of the main inhibitors to the planning process is the level of uncertainty faced by organisations. All organisations, whether in the private, voluntary or public sector have to face uncertainty, such as changes in legislation and changes in economic and social conditions. However, public sector organisations often consider they face more uncertainty than most.

The main causes of uncertainty can be summarised as follows:

The external environment
This uncertainty arises from factors that are outside the control of the organisation, such as, interest rates, changes in legislation, economic growth, and so on. Some of these changes can have a fundamental effect on the organisation, and in some extreme cases may cause it to reduce in size, merge with others, or become totally redundant and hence close.

The internal environment
This uncertainty arises from the way in which some organisations manage the planning process. This may include the timing of decisions, the allocation of resources, the sharing of information, and so on. The internal environment may also be affected by the way in which strategic decision making differs from operational decision making. For example, if the planning process is devolved to operational levels, but strategic decisions are made at the top of the organisation, the business plan may have to change to reflect organisational strategies which may not concur with operational ones.

The financial environment
This uncertainty may arise if the organisation does not know the exact amount of money it will receive in any one period. In the public sector this uncertainty is driven by a range of factors which include:

- *waiting for grant levels to be agreed*
- *having to generate sales/fees*
- *having income tied to performance targets, and so on*

Problem Solving

It is not uncommon for problems to arise during the business planning process. Typical problems can be summarised under the following headings:

Unclear vision
This can be a problem in many large organisations where there is a lack of corporate direction. In such circumstances departments, or service units, have to develop plans in isolation, and inconsistencies can emerge between departmental plans resulting in a lack of organisational synergy.

Disagreement with respect to the objectives
Where an organisation is led by a group of people rather than a single person, it is necessary to gain consensus regarding the objectives. This cannot always be achieved and hence the planning process can lack clear direction and drive, with the more innovative ideas being rejected and other objectives being watered down in order to obtain across the board agreement.

Disagreement with respect to the implementation strategies and/or actions
Even where there is agreement with respect to the aims and objectives of an organisation, there may be a number of ways in which those objectives might be achieved. As discussed, in chapter 6, there may be a range of available strategic options and the planning process can become difficult at this stage, if those involved in the development of the plan cannot agree on the way forward.

Insufficient funding or resources to deliver the plan

An important aspect of the planning process is the assumptions which are made. When the financial forecasts are developed, assumptions have to be made with respect to the business plan objectives and the plan's implementation. It is not uncommon to find that when this is done, there is insufficient income or other resources required to achieve the actions identified by the plan.

Lack of commitment to implementation

This problem tends to arise when the business plan has been developed by relatively few people in isolation from the rest of the organisation. This is often due to time constraints which do not allow for wide consultation, or a non-inclusive management style. If the majority of staff do not believe in the business plan, this may be reflected in a lack of commitment to fulfil the plan's strategies and actions.

Unpredicted change

It is impossible to accurately predict the future and hence any plan will be based on assumptions, some of which may be wrong. In addition, there will be changes that occur which are outside the organisation's control. These may cause problems with implementation or affect the aims and objectives.

To address some of these problems, the following strategies may be employed:

- *to have a high level of communication between all departments; it is important to try and co-ordinate the business planning process across departments and to establish some common ground even if there is no corporate vision or plan*

- *to link business planning to financial planning; there is normally a budget setting process which sets out certain financial parameters for the organisation as a whole. This gives a partial overall framework for planning*

- *to be prepared to accept majority decisions in some cases where consensus is not possible, and try to gain commitment to majority decisions*

- *to ensure the business plan is properly disseminated and channels provided through which people can influence the plan. It is also important to make everyone aware that the plan is not "set in stone", but is flexible and can evolve over time.*

- *to be prepared to amend the plan to accommodate changes such as restricted finances and resources. This will involve reviewing and in some cases revising the objectives, strategies and action plans.*

Summary

❑ The bottom up approach to business planning is where the lowest unit of operation produces a plan which is fed up into higher level plans, until the departmental and corporate plans are developed

❑ The top down approach to business planning is where the organisation sets out a strategic corporate plan as a framework within which all other departments/ divisions/ operational units need to formulate their individual plans

❑ Business planning should be an established cycle within the organisation and should, where possible, relate to the budgeting cycle

Exercise 10

Practical Problems of Planning

Using the information given for the prison in exercise 7, what will be the key problems encountered in developing a business plan?

Suggested solutions to this exercise can be found on page 117.

Exercise 11

Practical Problems of Planning

When undertaking the following activities, state the problems you have experienced to date and how they were or could be overcome:

a)   Developing a business/service plan

Problem	Solution
e.g. *agreeing objectives*	*e.g.* *organise awaydays*

b) Implementing a business/service plan

Problem	Solution
e.g. *finding time to complete actions*	*e.g.* *re-allocate tasks to others who may have time*

c)   Monitoring a business/service plan

Problem	Solution
e.g. *finding time to review actions*	*e.g* *.include monitoring as an agenda item at regular management meetings*

Chapter 8

FINANCIAL ASPECTS

A business plan should always include a financial section which outlines how the plan is to be financed. As stated in earlier chapters, business plans are regularly used as a fundraising tool. Even where the plan is not being used for fundraising purposes, it may have to be used to support a budget allocation.

Within the financial section it is usual to address some of the following issues:

- *Financial requirements - revenue and capital*
- *Unit costs*
- *Sources of finance*
- *Financial forecasts and assumptions*
- *Financial performance indicators*
- *Financial strategy*

Each of these areas are discussed in the following paragraphs.

Financial Requirements

The financial requirements set out the amount of money needed to implement the plan. This will include both revenue and capital costs. It is usual to distinguish between the two since they may be funded from different sources. In order to establish the financial requirements, it is best to develop financial forecasts identifying what needs to be spent each month across all expenditure headings.

An example of the above is where a business plan identifies the need to recruit an extra member of staff half way through the year at a salary of £20,000 per annum. The financial requirement for salaries is calculated by totalling all existing salaries and adding 50%, i.e. £10,000, of the new starter's salary. Other salary costs to be taken into account in the financial requirement will include increments, pay awards and employers on-costs.

The total requirement is constructed by considering all expenditure headings and making assumptions based on the business plan. The amounts used should be as accurate as possible with guess work kept to a minimum.

With respect to revenue expenditure, the financial requirement can be presented in various ways, however, the two most common presentations are shown in the following examples:

Example 1 - by expenditure heading

Organisation A states, in order to deliver their business plan it is necessary to finance the following:

	£
Salaries	*750,000*
Transport	*25,000*
Accommodation	*48,000*
Supplies and Services	*268,000*
Support Services	*63,000*
Central Recharges	*50,000*
TOTAL REQUIREMENT	*1,204,000*

Example 2 - by activity

	£
Advice giving	*400,000*
External visits to clients	*220,000*
Contract monitoring	*120,000*
Grants to third parties	*200,000*
Administration	*264,000*
TOTAL REQUIREMENT	*1,204,000*

A similar statement can be produced for capital expenditure. This would usually be broken down into the capital items, or activities that need to be undertaken during the year. In order for the financial requirement to be met, the capital expenditure of an organisation could be presented as follows:

	£
Purchase of new motor vehicles	*200,000*
Purchase of computer systems	*120,000*
Head office refurbishment	*180,000*
TOTAL CAPITAL REQUIREMENT	*500,000*

It is common place for the finance required to be greater than the finance available. In addition to this, there may be cash limits in operation which will restrict the amount of spending that can take place. The business plan needs to be formulated to realistically reflect these constraints. It may be possible to quantify the impact that the financial constraints have had on the planning process, and to identify the level of additional finance required to achieve a more ideal plan. This may give the organisation an opportunity to consider ways of either raising additional finance, or re-allocating resources to ensure certain service areas continue to be delivered.

Unit Costs

With value for money being a key aim for all public sector organisations, identifying unit costs for services has become increasingly important. Unit cost calculations are sometimes included in the financial section of the business plan, and provide the opportunity to link productivity/output to the financial input.

Using the previous example for the breakdown of the financial requirements across activity, unit costs can be stated as follows:

	Expected output	Expected unit cost	Total cost £
Advice giving	8,000 hours	£50 per hour	400,000
External visits to clients	1,000 visits	£220 per visit	220,000
Contract monitoring	120 contracts	£1,000 per contract	120,000
Grants to third parties	10 grants	£20,000 avg. grant	200,000
Administration	12,000 hours	£22 per hour	264,000
TOTAL REQUIREMENT			**1,204,000**

Output levels and unit costs can be established and used as performance targets. These can be monitored on a regular basis. Comparisons can be made year on year, or against other organisations, to ensure that value for money is being achieved. Where an organisation is not delivering value for money, this may become an objective to be achieved, and strategies and actions developed accordingly.

Sources of Finance

Regardless of the type of organisation, all financial requirements need to be met. Organisations use a range of different sources of finance which include:

Grants

This is the most usual source for public sector organisations. Grants are provided by central government, local government, specialist funding authorities and so on. A grant will tend to be for a specific period of time and relate to a particular activity. Grants are given for both capital and revenue expenditure.

Loans

Organisations tend to use loans to finance capital expenditure, and often the loan is secured against the capital item for which it is being used. It is quite common for public sector organisations to obtain loans from banks and other financial institutions to finance capital expenditure.

Overdrafts

All organisations need to have a bank account to conduct their financial affairs. As cash flows tend to fluctuate, there are occasions when there may be a need to use overdraft facilities to fund short term timing differences between payments for expenditure items and the receipt of income. Overdrafts can be used as a source of funding for revenue items.

Reserves

If at the end of a financial period an organisation creates surpluses or deficits, these are normally added to any brought forward surpluses thus creating accumulated surpluses to be carried forward. Accumulated surpluses can then be used to fund future expenditure on both revenue and capital items.

Investment capital

This is a source of funding which tends to be used mainly by private companies whereby individuals or companies invest funds in the organisation with a view to receiving a future return. With many of the changes now facing the public sector, the private sector is being encouraged to make such investments in public sector activities by working in partnership.

Donations

Many public sector organisations depend on this source of finance to contribute to their revenue finances. Donations can be given by companies, individuals, charitable organisations and so on. It is not untypical for some organisations to be the beneficiaries of legacies, or to receive a regular amount of money each year as a donation from a particular organisation interested in their work.

Fundraising

Fundraising can take many forms and includes applying for grants and obtaining donations. This has been identified as a separate source of funding as some organisations set out to undertake specific fundraising activities, these may include sponsorship activities, raffles, and so on.

Fees and charges

The main source of finance for most private sector organisations are the sales and fees generated with respect to the products and services they provide. In a similar way fees and charges are increasingly becoming an important source of income for the public sector.

Financial Forecasts and Assumptions

Financial forecasts will set out how expenditure and income will arise over the period of the business plan. It is normal to present financial forecasts on a monthly basis, however, some forecasts are presented quarterly. The business plan will tend to have forecasts for income and expenditure, and in some cases will have cash flow forecasts. An example of an income and expenditure forecast is illustrated as follows:

	Apr	May	Jun	Jul	Aug	Sep	Oct	Nov	Dec	Jan	Feb	Mar	Total
Income (£'000)													
Grant	250			250			250			250			1000
Fees	16	16	16	16	16	16	16	16	16	16	16	16	192
Donations				6					6				12
Total	266	16	16	272	16	16	266	16	22	266	16	16	1204
Expenditure (£'000)													
Salaries	62	62	62	62	62	62	63	63	63	63	63	63	750
Transport	2	2	2	2	2	2	2	2	2	2	2	3	25
Accommodation			12			12			12			12	48
Supplies & Services	22	22	23	22	22	23	22	22	23	22	22	23	268
Support Services			21				21				21		63
Central Recharges			5	5	5	5	5	5	5	5	5	5	50
Total	86	86	104	112	91	104	92	113	105	92	92	127	1204
Net Surplus/Deficit	180	-70	-88	160	-75	-88	174	-97	-83	174	-76	-111	0

This example shows that the sources of finance include grants, fees and donations. In this case the total required expenditure (£1,204,000) is fully met by the income (£1,204,000), thus creating a **balanced budget**. The forecast shows the timing of income and expenditure throughout the year. This can then be monitored to ensure that the organisation stays on target.

Financial Performance Indicators

The business plan will have objectives to be achieved and performance targets that have to be met. This may include financial performance indicators which tend to relate to the following:

- *Levels of surplus/deficit*
- *Reductions in expenditure achieved*
- *Increases in certain types of income*
- *Unit costs*
- *Return on capital*

For example, a service or business unit may only be able to justify its existence if it "breaks even", i.e. the income generated meets the total expenditure requirements. This financial performance indicator will, therefore, be crucial to the service's survival. Financial performance indicators are becoming more and more important to public sector organisations.

Financial Strategy

The financial strategy, like all other strategies in the business plan, should be supported by an action plan. The strategy will identify how the financial objectives and targets can be achieved. For example, part of the strategy may be to maximise the level of fees earned, and to monitor productivity to ensure target unit costs are being maintained. If this strategy is to be achieved there needs to be a specific action plan, as with the other strategies. The type of action plan in the above example may include calculating regular monthly targets for income generation and unit costs, and the production of a monthly monitoring report showing variances from the target.

Summary

❑ A business plan should always have a financial section showing how the plan is to be financed

❑ The financial requirements set out the amount of money needed in order to implement the plan

❑ With value for money being a key aim for all public services, looking at the unit costs has become increasingly important

❑ All financial requirements need to be met, regardless of the nature of the organisation. Some of the most common sources of finance include grants, loans and overdrafts

❑ Financial forecasts will set out how income and expenditure will arise over the period of the business plan. It is normal to present financial forecasts on a monthly basis, however, some forecasts are presented quarterly

❑ The business plan will have objectives to be achieved and performance targets that have to be met. This may include financial performance indicators

❑ The financial strategy should be supported by an action plan. This strategy will identify how the financial objectives and targets can be achieved

Exercise 12

Calculating the Financial Requirements

In order to establish the financial requirements for this year and how they should be met, a school has prepared a comprehensive business plan from which you have extracted the following key pieces of information.

a)   Last year's income and expenditure

	£'000
Grants	1,350
Fundraising	8
Donations	2
Charges	3
	1,363
Salaries	1,100
Supplies and Services	200
Support Services	50
Sundry Expenses	10
	1,360
Surplus for the year	3
Reserves b/f	10
Reserves c/f	13

b)   Financial implications of the plan

Staffing to remain the same with the addition of a part time staff member at £12,000 per year for an after school project. Parents contribute 50% of the total project cost, which will include £4,000 per annum sundry expenses in addition to the part time staff member's salary. These will be added to last year's charges which will be held constant

A pay award of 2% to be added to existing salaries

Fundraising to increase by 50%

Budget reductions of 2% on last year's totals to be achieved on all expenditure headings with the exception of sundry expenses where a saving of 20% is to be achieved

New books and equipment to be purchased from a special grant to reflect curriculum changes of £10,000

Staff training to take place at an additional cost of £8,000 for the year

Grant income will be frozen at last year's levels less the amount of the special grant for books and equipment. In addition, no increase in donations are expected

Complete the following from the information provided

THIS YEAR

Financial requirement is:

To be financed by:

Suggested solutions to this exercise can be found on page 118.

SOLUTIONS TO EXERCISES

Solutions to Exercises

Solution to Exercise 3
Developing a Business Plan

Given the position identified, the additional information required may include:

- Key assumptions that have been made

- Organisational structure and staff profiles

- Details of physical resources

- Details of any analysis undertaken such as sensitivity, risk assessment, SWOT and PEST analysis (see chapter 5)

- Market information on types of existing and potential users, competition with respect to proposed new ventures, etc.

- Financial information

  - Income and expenditure
  - Unit costs
  - Proposed fee levels

Solution to Exercise 5
Aims and Objectives

Stages in the Planning Process	AIM?	OBJECTIVE?
To provide a responsive service	✓	
To increase quality within financial constraints	✓	
To reduce waiting times by 4% during the year		✓
To increase income through a fair charging policy	✓	
To introduce means testing for non-essential services within the financial year		✓
To become the best service provider in the region	✓	
To improve response times to an average of 20 minutes next month		✓
To create a safer and cleaner environment	✓	
To create 10 new jobs every year		✓
To develop a quality service meeting the Requirements of international quality standards and obtaining ISO 9000 within the next 24 months		✓

Solution to Exercise 7
Undertaking a SWOT Analysis

Strengths	Weaknesses
• Clear management roles and responsibilities • Staff commitment • Wide range of activities offered • Good security systems • Good building condition • High levels of productivity	• Lack of financial resources • Lack of physical resources • Lack of planning • Poor communication • Irregular staff training
Opportunities	**Threats**
• Extension of facilities to provide more places • Improve conditions in prison • Increase staff training • Increase income from product sales	• Private sector competitors • Continuing cuts in budgets • Reduced staffing levels leading to reductions in quality and low staff morale

There are a number of areas that will critically affect the decision as to whether it is yes or no, these include:

a) The real position of the staff with respect to putting their jobs at risk in supporting the bid

b) The opportunities that may be on offer from some of the competitor organisations

c) The level of risk involved

d) The level of finance that may be required to mount a viable bid and how that finance could be raised

e) The likelihood of being able to protect jobs and /or make profits if the bid were to win

f) The ability of the management team to operate in a commercial environment

g) The scope for growth and long term survival

These points can be answered by undertaking research into:
~ the attitude of staff
~ competitors
~ the client base
~ the sector itself

Solution to Exercise 9
Developing Strategies

The following solution presents some illustrative points but is by no means exhaustive.

Service Development Strategy

- *Review current range of services for their effectiveness and continue to develop new initiatives which could attract alternative additional funding*

- *Identify alternative methods of service delivery that may use less resources*

- *Develop plan for the potential use of extra space should the prison be extended*

Marketing Strategy

- *Develop a promotional plan that raises the profile of the prison and presents all the positive achievements to date*

- *Gain commitment from staff and prisoners to act as advocates for the current regime*

Human Resource Strategy

- *Identify staff attitudes by undertaking research activities such as, questionnaires, interviews, etc.*

- *Develop a comprehensive training plan for all staff with an emphasis on maximising efficiency*

- *Consider scope for more flexible working by broadening skills*

Financial Strategy

- *Reduce net costs by increasing income from sales of goods and other funding sources*

- *Demonstrate value for money by showing unit costs and making comparisons with other similar institutions*

- *Prepare fundraising plans for extending the prison to accommodate more prisoners and enhancing the level of service*

Solution to Exercise 10
Practical Problems in Planning

From the information provided in exercise 7, some of the key problems in developing the business plan will include:

- Lack of time

- Lack of experience and expertise

- Lack of information

- Lack of research data on a range of areas

  - *competitors*
  - *staff*
  - *user feedback*
  - *client opinion*
  - *market place in general etc.*

- Lack of physical and financial resources

Solution to Exercise 12
Calculating the Financial Requirements

This year's financial requirement and sources of finance are calculated as follows:

The financial requirement is:

	(notes)	£'000
Salaries	(1)	1,112
Supplies and services	(2)	214
Support services		49
Sundry expenses	(3)	12
		1,387

To be financed by:

	(notes)	£'000
Grants	(4)	1,112
Special Grant		10
Fundraising		12
Donations		2
Charges	(5)	11
Reserves	(6)	12
		1,387

Notes:

1. Last year's salary (1,100) + 2% pay award (22) + part time staff member (12) - 2% budget reduction (22)

2. Last year's supplies and services (200) - 2% budget reduction (4) + new books and equipment (10) + staff training (8)

3. Last year's sundry expenses (10) - 20% budget reduction (2) + after school project sundries (4)

4. Last year's grant (1,350) - special grant (10)

5. Last year's charges (3) + parent contributions to 50% cost of after school project (8)

6. In order to meet the full financial requirement there is a need to utilise £12,000 from the reserves of £13,000

INDEX

A

B

C

D

E

F

H

I

K

L

M

O

P

Q

R

S

T

U

V

W

For further information see www.hbpublications.com
and www.fci-system.com

9 781899 448579